Insects &
Spiders

ISBN 1-74089-371-9
Colour reproduction by
Colourscan Overseas Co Pte Ltd
Printed by SNP Leefung Printers

Printed in China

DISCOVERIES

Insects & Spiders

CONSULTING EDITORS

George Else

& specialist staff
Department of Entomology
The Natural History Museum
London

WELDON OWEN

Contents

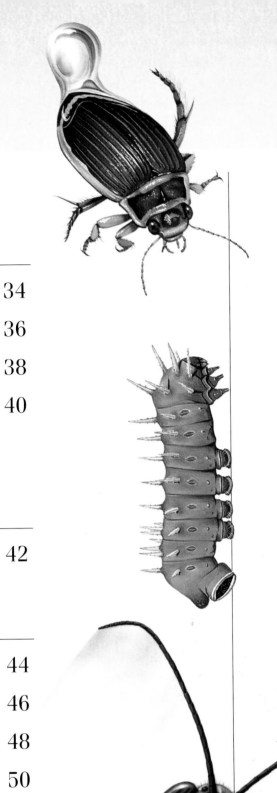

• THE BIG ORDERS •

• INSECTS AND PEOPLE •

• SPOTLIGHT ON SPIDERS •

The Great Success Story

Insects are among the most successful creatures in the living world. They first appeared more than 400 million years ago, and fossilised specimens, such as the dragonfly at left, show that some have changed little over this time. More than a million species of insect have been identified, which means that they outnumber all other animal species put together. Even more await discovery, and some scientists think that the total number of species may be as high as 10 million. There are several reasons for these tremendous numbers, but the most important is size. Because insects are so small, individuals need only tiny amounts of food. They eat many different things, including wood, leaves, blood and other insects, and they live in a great range of habitats. The survival of insects is also helped by the ability of some to fly, and by their ability to endure tough conditions. Some desert insects can cope with temperatures above 40˚C (104˚F), and many insect eggs can survive temperatures much colder than a freezer.

TAKING OFF
Insects were the first animals that were able to fly. Cockchafers use their wings to escape danger. This male may also fly far in search of a mate.

UNDERWATER INSECTS
Although insects are common in fresh water, hardly any are found in the sea. This diving beetle is one of many insects that live in fresh water.

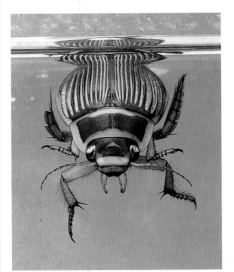

LIVING TOGETHER
Many insects gather in groups for part of their lives. This swarm of hungry locusts may have more than a billion individuals, who can munch through huge quantities of food.

THE INSECT ARMY
Scientists divide insects into about 30 different groups, called orders. Insects from some of the most important orders are shown here.

DID YOU KNOW?

Many insects are so light that gravity has little effect on them. They run up vertical surfaces almost as easily as they run down them. If they do lose their grip and fall, they are rarely injured when they hit the ground.

SMALL LIVING SPACES

The way insects are built means that their bodies need to be small and light, or they would become too heavy to move. As shown on this graph, most insect species are less than 25 mm (1 in) long. However, even long insects can still be very light. The goliath beetle weighs no more than 100 g (3½ ounces). Insects have turned being small into an advantage by exploiting places that are too cramped for larger animals. These places include the space between the upper and lower surfaces of leaves, and the tiny gaps among particles of soil.

Dwarf beetles
Some feather-winged beetles are only 0.25 mm (1/100 in) long. They feed on plant remains.

Earwigs
Earwigs usually measure about 25 mm (1 in) long, and make nests under bark or stones.

Giant beetles
The goliath beetle grows to 105 mm (4 in) long.

Number of species

Insect length in millimetres

Discover more in Insect Flight

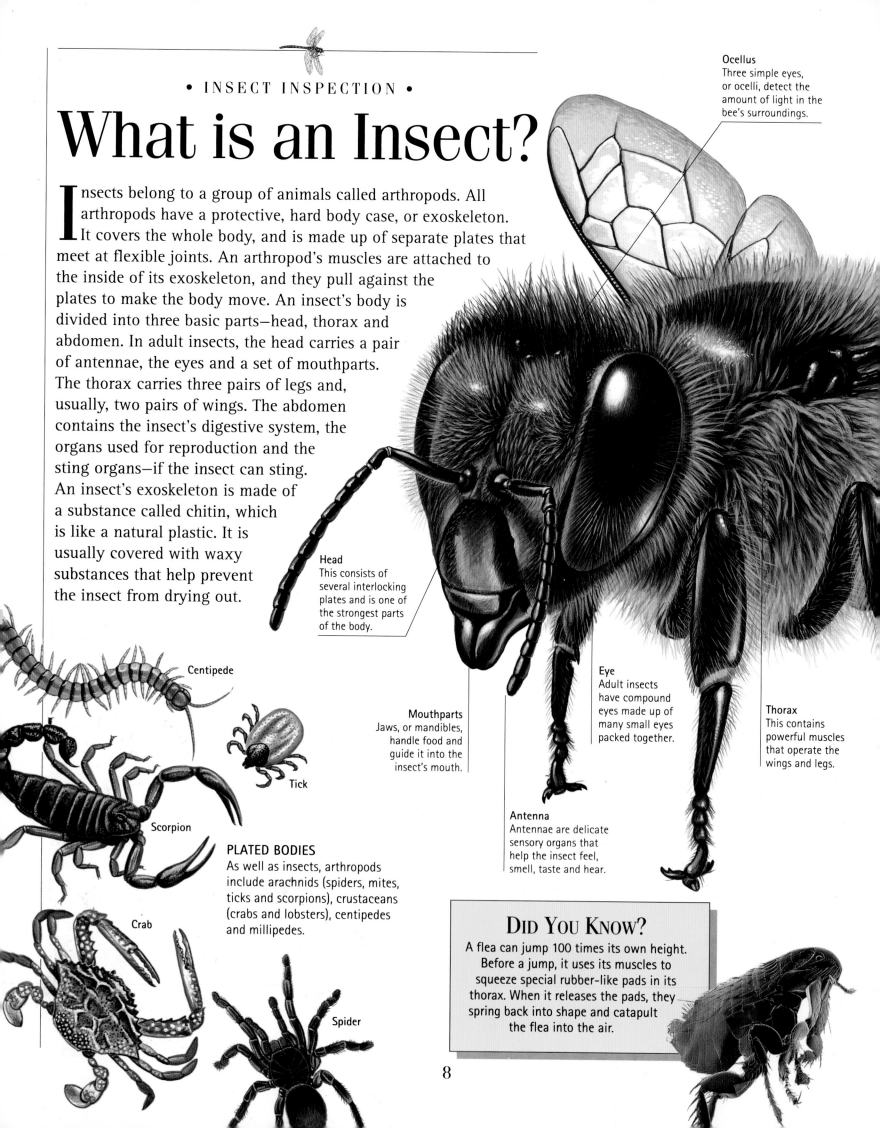

What is an Insect?

Insects belong to a group of animals called arthropods. All arthropods have a protective, hard body case, or exoskeleton. It covers the whole body, and is made up of separate plates that meet at flexible joints. An arthropod's muscles are attached to the inside of its exoskeleton, and they pull against the plates to make the body move. An insect's body is divided into three basic parts—head, thorax and abdomen. In adult insects, the head carries a pair of antennae, the eyes and a set of mouthparts. The thorax carries three pairs of legs and, usually, two pairs of wings. The abdomen contains the insect's digestive system, the organs used for reproduction and the sting organs—if the insect can sting. An insect's exoskeleton is made of a substance called chitin, which is like a natural plastic. It is usually covered with waxy substances that help prevent the insect from drying out.

Ocellus
Three simple eyes, or ocelli, detect the amount of light in the bee's surroundings.

Head
This consists of several interlocking plates and is one of the strongest parts of the body.

Centipede

Tick

Scorpion

Crab

Spider

Mouthparts
Jaws, or mandibles, handle food and guide it into the insect's mouth.

Eye
Adult insects have compound eyes made up of many small eyes packed together.

Thorax
This contains powerful muscles that operate the wings and legs.

Antenna
Antennae are delicate sensory organs that help the insect feel, smell, taste and hear.

PLATED BODIES
As well as insects, arthropods include arachnids (spiders, mites, ticks and scorpions), crustaceans (crabs and lobsters), centipedes and millipedes.

DID YOU KNOW?

A flea can jump 100 times its own height. Before a jump, it uses its muscles to squeeze special rubber-like pads in its thorax. When it releases the pads, they spring back into shape and catapult the flea into the air.

REPEATING PATTERN
An insect's body is made up of plates arranged in segments. These segments are easy to see on the abdomen of this cockroach.

Wing
Insect wings are supported by thickened veins. The pattern of veins varies in different insects.

PRIMITIVE INSECT
A silverfish does not have wings or ocelli. Its flattened body allows it to wriggle into small crevices, even between the pages of a book.

Abdomen
More flexible than the head or thorax, this expands when the insect feeds.

Leg
In some insects, the three pairs of legs are very different in size. They are all attached to the thorax.

Foot
Hooks, pads and suckers on the feet allow insects to cling onto surfaces or to catch food.

A TYPICAL INSECT
A worker honeybee is a typical flying insect, with two pairs of wings and six legs. Its body is divided into three basic parts, the head, thorax and abdomen.

NEW SKINS

Our skeleton grows in step with the rest of our body, but once an insect's exoskeleton has hardened, it cannot become any larger. In order to grow, the insect has to moult, or shed, its "skin", and replace it with a new one. During moulting, the old exoskeleton splits open and the insect crawls out. The insect then takes in air or water, so that its body expands before the new exoskeleton becomes hard. Some insects moult more than 25 times, while others moult just twice. Once an insect becomes an adult, it usually stops moulting and does not grow any more.

Discover more in Getting Started

9

A Closer View

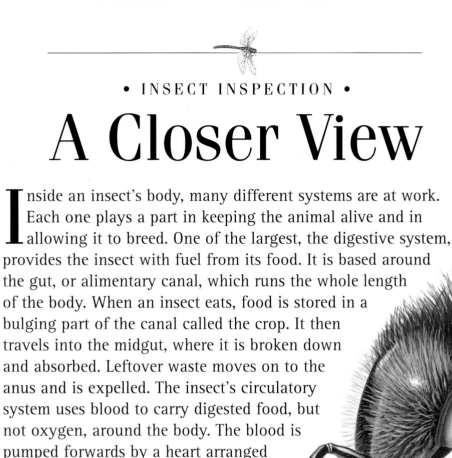

Sensing the surroundings
A honeybee's exoskeleton is covered with tiny hairs that detect the slightest air current. Each hair sends signals to the brain.

Trachea

Inside an insect's body, many different systems are at work. Each one plays a part in keeping the animal alive and in allowing it to breed. One of the largest, the digestive system, provides the insect with fuel from its food. It is based around the gut, or alimentary canal, which runs the whole length of the body. When an insect eats, food is stored in a bulging part of the canal called the crop. It then travels into the midgut, where it is broken down and absorbed. Leftover waste moves on to the anus and is expelled. The insect's circulatory system uses blood to carry digested food, but not oxygen, around the body. The blood is pumped forwards by a heart arranged along a muscular tube, but it flows back again through the body spaces among the body organs. The nervous system and the brain ensure that all the other systems work together. They collect signals from the sense organs, and carry messages from one part of the body to another.

Control centre
An insect's brain collects signals from the eyes and other sense organs, and coordinates its body. It is connected to the nerve cord.

Power plant
The muscles in the thorax power the bee's wings and the legs. Like all the bee's muscles, they are bathed in blood.

Mini-brain
Swellings, called ganglia, are arranged at intervals along the nerve cord. These control sections of the body.

Liquid meals
The bee uses its tongue like a drinking straw to suck up sugary nectar from flowers.

GETTING A GRIP
Each fly's foot has a pair of claws and bristly pads. The claws allow the fly to grip rough surfaces, while the bristly pads help it to cling onto smooth surfaces.

INSIDE A BEE
This illustration shows major body systems of the worker honeybee. The digestive system is coloured cream, the respiratory system white, the nervous system grey and the circulatory system green.

Air intakes
Openings, called spiracles, let air into the bee's internal air tubes (tracheae). Each spiracle has hairs to keep out dust and water.

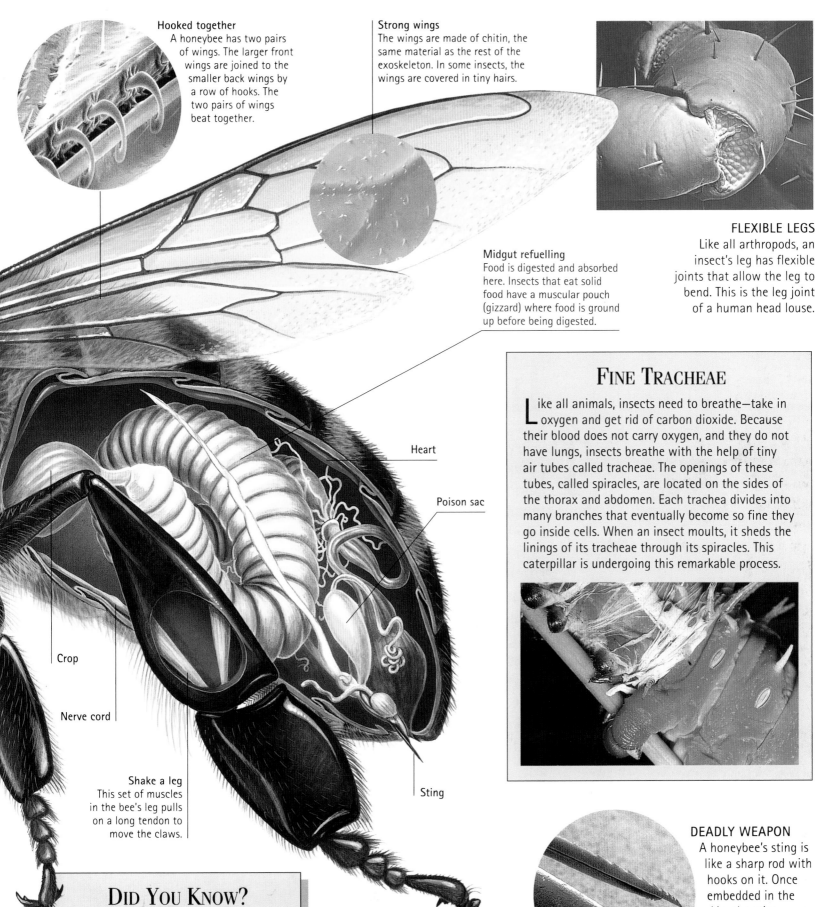

Hooked together
A honeybee has two pairs of wings. The larger front wings are joined to the smaller back wings by a row of hooks. The two pairs of wings beat together.

Strong wings
The wings are made of chitin, the same material as the rest of the exoskeleton. In some insects, the wings are covered in tiny hairs.

FLEXIBLE LEGS
Like all arthropods, an insect's leg has flexible joints that allow the leg to bend. This is the leg joint of a human head louse.

Midgut refuelling
Food is digested and absorbed here. Insects that eat solid food have a muscular pouch (gizzard) where food is ground up before being digested.

Heart

Poison sac

Crop

Nerve cord

Shake a leg
This set of muscles in the bee's leg pulls on a long tendon to move the claws.

Sting

FINE TRACHEAE

Like all animals, insects need to breathe—take in oxygen and get rid of carbon dioxide. Because their blood does not carry oxygen, and they do not have lungs, insects breathe with the help of tiny air tubes called tracheae. The openings of these tubes, called spiracles, are located on the sides of the thorax and abdomen. Each trachea divides into many branches that eventually become so fine they go inside cells. When an insect moults, it sheds the linings of its tracheae through its spiracles. This caterpillar is undergoing this remarkable process.

DID YOU KNOW?

All insects are protected by body cases, but in larvae (grubs) the case is often quite thin. These lily beetle larvae shield themselves from their enemies with a protective coat made from their own droppings.

DEADLY WEAPON
A honeybee's sting is like a sharp rod with hooks on it. Once embedded in the skin, the sting releases its poison. Here, the sting (top) is compared to a needle.

Discover more in Insect Defence

SENSORY SKILLS

The shape of antennae varies among insects, and sometimes even between males and females of the same species.

Night-time feeder
A long-horned beetle's long antennae are used for feeling its way in the dark.

Seeking a mate
In flight, a male cockchafer's antennae open out to detect the scent of a female.

Damp skin spots
The human louse uses its antennae to sense damp parts of a body where it feeds on blood.

Air detector
Each butterfly antenna is a slender shaft ending with a small knob. The shafts are covered with hairs that detect air currents.

Hot spots
A female mosquito's feathery antennae sense heat from warm-blooded animals. This enables her to find food in the dark.

Feathery sniffer
A male emperor moth can smell a female more than 3 km (2 miles) away.

Insect Senses

To survive, an insect has to know about the world around it. It must be able to find food, track down a mate and, most important of all, be able to detect its enemies before they have a chance to attack. Like many other animals, insects have five main senses—sight, hearing, smell, touch and taste. Each type of insect specialises in using some of these senses more than others. Because dragonflies and horseflies fly during the day, they have large eyes that help them find their victims. Most moths, on the other hand, fly at night. Instead of using sight, they find their food and partners by smell. As well as using senses to find out about the world, insects also have senses that monitor their own bodies. These tell them which way up they are flying, how their wings and legs are positioned, and whether they are speeding up or slowing down. For flying insects, these senses are particularly important.

Human's view

Bee's view

SEEING THE INVISIBLE
Many insects see wavelengths of light that are invisible to us. Above right is how a bee may view a flower. It gives more detail than a human view and guides the bee to the nectar.

Simple eyes
Known as ocelli, these small eyes on the top of the head sense the difference between sunlight and shade.

SMALL EYES
The more eyelets an insect has, the more clearly it sees. This wingless worker ant lives in the dark and has small compound eyes, which contain only a few hundred eyelets.

Feeling the heat
A horsefly's antennae are sensitive to heat, and are used to locate areas of exposed skin on a warm-blooded animal.

Making up a picture
The horsefly's compound eyes each contain several thousand eyelets. The fly's brain combines the signals from the eyelets to make up an image of the surroundings.

LOOKING FOR BLOOD
Female horseflies feed on blood, and they rely mainly on vision to track down a meal. Like most insects, they have compound eyes, which are made of many smaller eyes, called eyelets, packed tightly together.

Taste bud | Hair

MULTIPURPOSE ANTENNAE
This magnified picture shows the surface of a wasp's antenna. These antennae carry taste buds for sensing food, sensors that smell the air, and hairs that respond to touch.

Smell sensor

EARS ON THE BODY
Insects often use their antennae to hear, but they also have other ways of detecting different sounds and vibrations.

Ears on legs
Bush crickets have ears on their front legs. Each ear is a thin oval membrane that moves when the air vibrates.

Feeling the ground
Ants sense vibrations through their legs. They often respond to these vibrations by preparing to attack an enemy.

Ears on the abdomen
Grasshoppers and locusts have ears on their abdomen. They are particularly sensitive to the calls made by their own species.

Leg bristles
A cockroach uses special bristles to sense the vibrations made by something moving towards it.

Wings as ears
The thin and delicate wings of a lacewing pick up vibrations in the air and sense movements.

Discover more in Insect Flight

LIVING DRILL
The hazelnut weevil has a long, slender "snout" with tiny jaws at the tip. Using its jaws like a drill, the weevil chews holes in hazelnuts.

Food and Feeding

I ndividually, insects are quite choosy about what they eat, but together they devour a vast range of different foods. Many insects feed on plants or on small animals, but some survive on more unusual food, including rotting wood, blood, horns or even wool. To tackle each of these foods, insects have a complicated set of specially shaped mouthparts. A praying mantis, for example, has sharp jaws, or mandibles, that stab and cut up its captives, while its other mouthparts help to hold the food and pass it towards the mouth. A grasshopper has similar mouthparts, but its main jaws are much stronger and blunter, and so are ideal for crushing the plant material it prefers. The mouthparts of insects that feed on liquids often look very different than those of insects that live on solid foods. A mosquito has a long stylet that works like a syringe, while a butterfly or moth has a long tongue, or proboscis, which acts like a drinking straw. As this butterfly (above left) demonstrates, the tongue conveniently coils up when not in use.

MIDAIR REFUELLING
With its tongue uncoiled, a hawk moth drinks nectar from deep inside a flower. Some hawk moths have tongues that are more than 15 cm (6 in) long.

CHANGING TASTES
Larvae and adult insects often eat very different foods. An adult potter wasp feeds on nectar whereas its larva (left top) feeds on caterpillars.

INSECT MOUTHPARTS

I nsect mouthparts are like tools in a toolkit. They are specially shaped to gather particular food and allow it to be swallowed.

Spongy pads
Houseflies use a spongy pad to pour saliva over their food. After the food has dissolved, it is sucked up.

Piercing mouthparts
Female mosquitoes use their needle-like mouthparts to stab through the skin and suck up blood. Males sip only plant juices.

Powerful jaws
Many ants have strong jaws for gripping and cutting up small animals. Some can slice through human skin.

FAST FOOD
A locust chops through a tasty leaf quickly. Its mouthparts, called palps, explore the leaf as it eats.

DID YOU KNOW?

This darkling beetle lives in Africa's Namib Desert, where the only moisture comes from mist rolling in from the sea. To get water, the beetle points its abdomen into the wind, and collects the moisture that condenses on its body.

MOPPING UP

Before it can eat, a housefly must pour saliva over its food. The saliva often dries to form small spots that can be seen after the fly has moved on.

PATIENT KILLER

A praying mantis surprises its victims by striking out with its front legs. The legs snap shut and help grip the prey with sharp spines. The mantis often begins to feed even while its catch is still struggling to escape.

FEROCIOUS TWIG
Most caterpillars eat plants for food, but this looper moth caterpillar catches other insects. Camouflaged to look like a twig, it attacks small flies when they land nearby.

DEADLY DASH
After cockroaches, tiger beetles are among the fastest sprinters of the insect world. Moving at more than 0.5 m (1½ ft) per second, this tiger beetle is chasing some ants. The beetle's large jaws will quickly snatch and crush the ants.

• STAYING ALIVE •

Predators and Parasites

One third of all insects feed on other animals, either as predators or parasites. Predators catch their prey by hunting it actively, or lying in wait until food comes within reach. Some of the most spectacular hunters feed in the air. Dragonflies, for example, swoop down and snatch up other flying insects with their long legs. On the ground, active hunters include fast-moving beetles, as well as many ants and wasps. Some wasps specialise in hunting spiders, which they sting—sometimes after a fierce battle. Insects that hunt by stealth, or lying in wait, are usually harder to spot. These include mantises and bugs, which are often superbly camouflaged to match their background. A few of these stationary hunters build special traps to catch their food. Antlion larvae dig steep-sided pits in loose soil and wait for ants to tumble in. Insects that are parasites live on or inside another animal, called the host, and feed on its body or blood. The host animal can sometimes be harmed or killed.

EASY PICKINGS
Hunting is sometimes easy work. Because aphids move very slowly, they cannot escape hungry ladybirds.

UNDERWATER ATTACK
Only a few insects are large enough to kill vertebrates (animals with backbones). This diving beetle has managed to catch a salamander.

DEATH OF A BEE
Assassin bugs use their sharp beak to stab their victims and then suck out the body fluids. This one has caught a honeybee by lying in wait inside a flower.

CLEANING UP

Instead of hunting live animals, burying beetles feed on dead bodies. They bury carcasses, then feed themselves and their larvae on the remains.

DINING IN

Parasitic insects use living animals as fresh food. Many lay their eggs on the larvae of other insects, or inject eggs through the skin of the victim. When the eggs hatch, these larvae feed on their host. They start with the less essential parts of the host's body, so that it survives for as long as possible. Eventually, they burst out through the host's skin and turn into adults. This hawk moth caterpillar has been feasted on by parasitic wasps, and is covered with their empty cocoons.

DID YOU KNOW?

The larvae of fungus gnats, found in caves in New Zealand, catch flying insects by glowing in the dark. Each larva produces a thread of sticky mucus that traps insects as they fly towards the glowing light. The larva then eats the insect and the trap.

Insects and Plants

When insects first appeared on Earth, they found a world brimming with plants. Over millions of years, insects and plants evolved side by side. During this time, some insects became deadly enemies of plants, but others became valuable partners in the struggle for survival. Insects use plants for many things, but the most important of all is for food. Different insects eat all parts of plants, from roots and stems to leaves and flowers. Most of them eat living plants, but some help to break down plants once they are dead. By doing this, insects help to recycle important nutrients so that other plants can use them. Insects also live on or in plants, and they often damage plants when they set up home. Despite this insect attack, plants are not completely defenceless. Many use sticky hairs or chemicals to keep insects away, and some even catch insects and digest them. However, not all visitors are unwelcome. When bees feed at flowers, they carry pollen from plant to plant. This helps plants to pollinate and spread to new areas.

FLYING COURIER
Bees, butterflies, moths and wasps are all common visitors to flowers. These insects become dusted with pollen while they feed on the sugary nectar of the flowers.

GETTING A GRIP
Caterpillars have to hang on tight while they feed. They do this with special "legs" that end in sucker-like pads. They lose these legs when they become moths or butterflies.

BREAKING OUT
Seeds are packed with stores of food that help young plants to survive. This weevil climbing out of a grain of wheat has just finished eating some of these nutrients.

SLOW GROWTH
The larva of a stag beetle spends its entire early life hidden inside rotting wood. Because wood is not very nutritious, it takes the larva a long time to mature.

STRANGE BUT TRUE
The caterpillars of one Mexican moth grow inside the beans of a small bush. If a bean falls onto warm, sunny ground, the caterpillar inside jerks its body to make the bean "jump" into the shade. Each bean can move up to 5 cm (2 in) in a single hop.

LEAFY FEAST
Eating side by side, beetle larvae chew away at a leaf. Insects kill some plants, but enough plants are always left to allow both plants and insects to survive.

BUILDING WITH LEAVES
Female leafcutter bees clip out pieces of leaf with their jaws, and take the pieces back to their nests. They use them to make tube-shaped cells for larvae.

PLANTS THAT EAT INSECTS
In order to grow, plants need substances called nutrients. They usually get these from the ground, but some plants that live where nutrients are scarce also get them from the bodies of insects. This sundew has trapped a fly in its sticky hairs, and will soon digest its prey. Other carnivorous plants catch insects in fluid-filled traps, or with leaves that suddenly snap shut.

19

Insect Defence

For insects, the world is full of danger. They are under constant threat of being eaten, and their enemies include not only birds, lizards and spiders, but also other insects. Many insects defend themselves by hurrying away at the first sign of trouble. Others stay still and well hidden. They hide in soil or rotting wood, or make themselves look like the objects around them. Some insects imitate thorns, sticks, leaves and even animal droppings, and they are often invisible until they move. Another line of defence works in a completely different way. Instead of hiding, some insects are brightly coloured and easy to see, like the caterpillar on the left. But their colours warn predators that they are unpleasant or even dangerous to eat. Insects like this, however, are not always what they seem. Some harmless insects imitate ones that have a bad taste, and others look just like ones with a dangerous sting. If all these defences fail, some insects stand their ground and attack. With their armoured bodies, sharp jaws and toxic chemicals, they often live to fight another day.

Mottled beauty
With wings spread out, the moth blends into the tree bark.

Bark bug
This has a flat, patterned body like the surface of tree bark.

Leaf insect
The flattened body and forewings mimic a single leaf.

Stick insect
Slow movements help a stick insect to look like part of a plant.

Sword-grass butterfly caterpillar
The caterpillar's slender green body is well hidden among blades of grass.

BATTLE POSTURE
This wood ant prepares for battle by thrusting its abdomen upwards. When an attacker comes closer, the ant squirts it with a stream of acid from the tip of its abdomen.

SICKLY SCENT
When some insects, such as this bush cricket, are threatened, they ooze droplets of a liquid that has a repulsive smell. Attackers usually stay away.

Comma butterfly
Ragged brown wings imitate the colour and shape of dead leaves.

Long-headed grasshopper
The grasshopper's pointed head gives it a sticklike outline.

BLENDING IN
Insects are experts in the art of camouflage. This scene shows how 13 different insects use camouflage to avoid being spotted.

STARING EYES
Many moths have two large spots on their back wings. When disturbed, they reveal the spots, which look like two eyes set in a menacing face.

Emerald moth caterpillar
The body projections make this caterpillar look like a twig with buds.

Swallowtail butterfly larva
The texture and shape of the larva's body look like bird droppings.

Bush cricket
The veined front wings are pressed together to look like an upright leaf.

DEFENSE PLANS
There is no such thing as one completely successful defence plan. Many insects have several ways to defend themselves. If one method is not successful, they will try another. The puss moth caterpillar relies initially on camouflage, but if an attacker sees it, the caterpillar moves onto the next plan. This involves inflating its head, and producing a pair of "horns" to frighten its attacker. If the caterpillar is still in danger, it squirts a spray of acid at its attacker, from a gland just beneath the head.

Flower mantis
This mantis is the same colour as the flower. It is disguised as it waits to catch prey.

Angle shades moth
The wings look like a newly fallen leaf.

Cryptic grasshopper
The round outline and mottled colours imitate a small pebble.

KICKING BACK
The giant weta from New Zealand raises its powerful back legs to show that it can fight back. These legs have large spines.

DANGEROUS MOMENT
Male insects are often smaller than females and some have to be careful when they mate. Unless he is careful, this male mantis will end up as a meal for his partner.

FOOD FOR THE YOUNG
Insects often use their sense of smell to find good places for their eggs. This dead mouse has attracted blowflies that are ready to lay eggs.

Getting Started

Animals begin life in two different ways. Some develop inside their mother's body until they are ready to be born. Others, including most insects, develop from eggs outside their mother's body. Before a female insect can lay her eggs, she normally has to mate. Once this has happened, she chooses a place for her eggs, making sure that each one is near a source of suitable food. In most cases, she then abandons them, and makes no attempt to look after her young. However, not all insects start life this way. A few female insects can reproduce without needing to mate. Some insects give birth to live young, such as aphids who give birth to nymphs, and tsetse flies who give birth to larvae. A few insects are careful parents and take care of their eggs. Female earwigs lay small clutches of eggs and look after them by licking them clean. Many bugs carry their eggs on their backs, and guard their young after they hatch.

A QUEEN'S LIFE
In an ant colony, only one individual—the queen—lays eggs. The eggs are carried away by worker ants, who tend and feed the young after they hatch. Most termites also reproduce this way.

DID YOU KNOW?
Insects that give birth to live young have fast-growing families. Within a few days, a female leaf beetle or aphid can be surrounded by dozens of offspring. Unlike insects that start life as eggs, each one can feed straight away.

EGGS ON THE MOVE
A female giant water bug glues her eggs onto the back of a male. While carrying the eggs, the male is unable to use his wings.

INSECT EGGS

Insect eggs are remarkable objects. Because they are so small, it is often difficult to see them without a microscope. A few insects drop their eggs from the air, but most glue them firmly to something that will provide food for their young. Insect eggs are sometimes laid singly, but many are laid in clusters, with hundreds or even thousands of eggs side by side. A few insects make special structures to help their eggs survive. Cockroaches lay batches of eggs in special cases; green lacewings lay their eggs on slender stalks, which makes the eggs difficult for predators to reach. Some eggs hatch soon after they are laid, but others stay inactive during months of cold or dry weather, when all the adults may die.

Horsefly eggs

Eucalyptus tip bug eggs

Cockroach egg case

Green lacewing eggs

A GOOD START
This female ichneumon wasp drills into a tree branch. She stings the larva of a wood wasp and deposits an egg through the tube, or ovipositor, onto the larva. When this egg hatches, it will feed on its unlucky host.

From Nymph to Adult

After an insect has hatched out of its egg, it starts to feed and grow. However, as well as growing, it often changes shape. This is called metamorphosis. In some insects, the changes are only slight, so the young insect looks quite like the adult form. In others, the changes are so great that the young and adult look completely different. Insects that change only slightly include dragonflies, grasshoppers, earwigs, cockroaches, true bugs and praying mantises. Their young are called nymphs. A nymph does not have wings, although it does have small wing buds, and it is usually a different colour from its parents. It often lives in a different habitat and feeds on different food. Most nymphs will moult several times. Each time a nymph sheds its skin, its body gets bigger and its wing buds become longer. Eventually, the nymph is ready for its final moult. It breaks out of its old skin, and emerges as an adult insect with working wings. It can then fly away to find a mate.

FINAL MOULT
After many years feeding underground as nymphs, these cicadas are shedding their skins for the last time. Their crumpled wings will soon expand and dry.

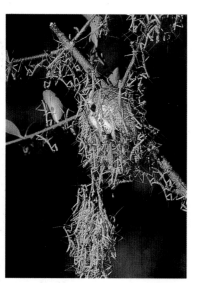

MANTIS MARCH
These newly hatched praying mantis nymphs look like miniature versions of their parents. They have well-developed legs, but their wing buds are still very small.

UNDERWATER NYMPHS
Adult dragonflies live in the air, but their nymphs develop under the water. Each nymph lives in water for up to five years before it hauls itself up a plant stem, sheds its skin for the last time, and emerges as an adult, able to fly.

Laying eggs
This dragonfly inserts her eggs into a water plant. Some species let the eggs fall to the bottom of ponds.

On the move
Dragonfly eggs can take several weeks to hatch. Each tiny nymph chews its way out of its egg case.

NYMPH TO ADULT
Like their parents (far right), nymphs have six legs. Their bodies change in proportion as they grow, but they keep the same overall shape.

Box elder bug

Desert locust

Earwig

BRIEF LIFE
This female mayfly has spent up to three years as a nymph, but will live for just one day as an adult. She cannot eat or drink, and her only purpose is to mate and lay eggs.

BREATHING UNDERWATER

Many insects spend a large part of their lives underwater. They all have to breathe, but they do so in different ways. Water scorpions and mosquito larvae get oxygen from the air, breathing through tubes that pierce the surface. Diving beetles and back swimmers collect bubbles of air at the surface, and carry them underwater when they swim. Dragonfly and damselfly nymphs use special flaps called gills to get their oxygen from the water. In dragonflies, the gills are inside the nymph's abdomen, but in damselflies, they stick out like small tails.

Water scorpion

Diving beetle

Damselfly nymph

On patrol
An adult dragonfly has large eyes and is a powerful flier. It swoops over the water and catches other insects.

Drying time
The newly emerged adult rests in the sunshine while its wings expand and dry out.

Mating
A male (top left) and female come together to mate. Gripping the female just behind her head, the male fertilises her eggs.

Leaving the water
Just before its final moult, the nymph climbs up a plant stem and out of the water.

Breaking out
The nymph swallows air to burst its old skin, and then eases itself out.

Hunter's diet
Using its special hinged jaws, the nymph catches tadpoles, worms and even small fish.

STRANGE BUT TRUE

In the United States there are two species of cicada that take either 13 or 17 years to mature underground. In response to some mysterious signal, millions of adults emerge together. They mate and lay eggs, and the cycle is repeated again.

A CHANGE OF LIFE
The atlas moth has four stages in its life cycle—egg, larva, pupa and adult. Larvae put all their energy into feeding, while adults mate and lay eggs.

Mating
A female's scent attracts a male, and the moths mate.

Laying eggs
The female moth searches for suitable food plants and glues her eggs to the leaves.

The next stage
A larva, or caterpillar, hatches from an egg. It grows bigger with several moults.

DID YOU KNOW?
Most larvae feed for many hours every day, and they put on weight very quickly. Just before they turn into pupae, fully grown larvae are often heavier than the adult insects of the same species.

LEGLESS LARVAE
Mosquito larvae live in water and feed on microscopic animals. They swim by wriggling their bodies, and breathe through short tubes.

• CYCLES OF LIFE •

A Complete Change

Many young insects look quite unlike their parents. They do not have wings, and some do not even have legs. They often spend all their time on, or in, the things they eat. Young insects such as these are called larvae, and they include maggots, grubs and caterpillars. Compared to adult insects, they have soft bodies. Larvae protect themselves by tasting horrible, by being difficult to swallow, or by hiding away. A typical larva feeds for several weeks, shedding its skin several times while growing. When mature, its appetite suddenly vanishes, it stops moving and it becomes a pupa. The pupa has a tough outer case, and is sometimes protected by a silk cocoon. Inside the case, the larva's body changes dramatically. It is broken down and reassembled, so that it gradually turns into an adult insect. When this change, or metamorphosis, is complete, the case splits open and the adult insect, with wings, breaks out. It is now ready to reproduce.

Pupating
The caterpillar fastens itself in position with threads of silk.

Opening up
After breaking open the pupal case, the adult moth pumps blood into its wings.

Airborne
When its wing veins have hardened, the moth flies off.

NATURAL SILK
Each silk moth cocoon is made of a single silk thread more than 1 km ($\frac{1}{2}$ mile) long. As soon as a moth emerges from its cocoon, it mates.

PAMPERED UPBRINGING
Honeybee larvae mature inside wax cells, and worker bees bring food to them. These bees are turning into pupae, and will soon emerge as adults.

TIME FOR A CHANGE

Insects that change completely when they mature have four stages in their life cycles. Each stage usually lasts for a different length of time and these times vary from species to species. The stag beetle is a relatively slow developer, and spends many months as a larva hidden in wood, feeding only on rotting vegetation. The ladybird develops more quickly, and spends over half its life as an adult. The northern caddis fly spends most of its life as a larva. It lives in ponds and quiet waters in a specially constructed case.

Stag beetle

Ladybird

Caddis fly

0 years	1	2	3	4

☐ Egg   ☐ Larva   ☐ Pupa   ☐ Adult

Discover more in The Great Success Story

27

Insect Flight

Insects were the first animals to fly. Today they share the air with birds and bats, but they are still the most numerous fliers in the animal world. Some insects fly on their own. Others, such as midges and locusts, gather in swarms. A swarm can contain just a few dozen insects, or more than a billion. Flying allows insects to escape from danger, and makes it easier for them to find mates. It is also a perfect way to reach food. Bees and butterflies fly among flowers, and hawk moths often hover in front of them. Dragonflies use flight to attack other insects in the air. They are the fastest fliers in the insect world, and can reach speeds of more than 50 km (31 miles) per hour. Most insects have two pairs of wings, made of the same material that covers the rest of their bodies. The wings are powered by muscles in the thorax. These muscles either flap the wings directly, or make the thorax move and this causes the wings to flap.

WINGS COMPARED
In most insects, the front and back wings look different. Insect wings are supported by branching veins, and are sometimes covered with tiny hairs or scales.

Pleated back wings
The back wings of a mantis fold up like fans when not in use.

DID YOU KNOW?
Insects such as thrips and aphids are too small and slow to make much headway on their own. Instead, they are carried by the wind, blowing them from one place to another far away.

VERTICAL TAKEOFF
Butterflies rest with their wings together. At takeoff, the wings peel apart, and the air sucks the butterfly upwards and away from danger.

REFUELLING STOP
Flight is a fast and efficient way of getting about, but it uses a lot of energy. Many insects, such as bees, drink sugary nectar from flowers to give them energy.

LONG-DISTANCE TRAVELLERS

Although insects are small animals, some of them travel huge distances in search of food or warmth. Dragonflies, locusts and moths often migrate, but the star travellers of the insect world are butterflies. In spring, North American monarch butterflies (left) set off northwards from Mexico. Many travel more than 2,400 km (1,500 miles). Painted lady butterflies set out from North Africa, and often make even longer journeys. Some of them manage to cross the Arctic Circle in Scandinavia, making a total distance of more than 2,900 km (1,800 miles).

Single pair of wings
Instead of back wings, true flies have tiny knobs called halteres.

Plumed wings
Thrips and plume moths have wings that look like tiny feathers.

Hooked wings
A wasp's back and front wings are connected to each other by tiny hooks.

Double pair of wings
A dragonfly's front and back wings beat in opposite directions.

ASSISTED TAKEOFF
Weak fliers, such as this scorpion fly, often jump into the air from a high point. This assists them in gaining lift during takeoff.

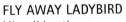

FLY AWAY LADYBIRD
Like all beetles, a ladybird has hardened front wings that do not beat up and down. They provide lift that helps the ladybird stay in the air.

Takeoff!
The front wings swing outwards, and when the back wings are beating fast enough, the ladybird takes off.

Making ready
Before it can fly, a ladybird opens its front wings and unfolds its back wings.

Grounded
A ladybird's back wings are normally packed away under its hard front wings.

LOOPING WALK

Some caterpillars move by holding the ground tight with their front legs, and pulling their body into a loop. They stretch forwards to straighten the loop, and then start the process again.

• AN INSECT'S WORLD •

Moving Around

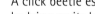

Many people find insects alarming because of their sudden movements. Insects are not always fast, but because they weigh so little, most of them can stop and start far more suddenly than we can. The way an insect moves depends on where it lives. On land, the slowest movers are legless larvae. They have to wriggle to get about. Adult insects normally move using their legs, and they either walk or run, or jump into the air. The champion jumpers of the insect world are grasshoppers and crickets, but jumping insects also include fleas, froghoppers and some beetles. Tiny, wingless insects called springtails also jump, but instead of using their legs, they launch themselves by flicking a special "tail". Legs are useful in water, and insects have evolved a variety of leg shapes to suit watery ways of life. Water boatmen and diving beetles have legs like oars, and row their way through the water. Pond-skaters live on top of the water, and have long and slender legs that spread their weight over the surface.

HEAD-BANGER

A click beetle escapes danger by lying on its back and keeping perfectly still (above left). If attacked, its head suddenly snaps upwards, hurling it out of harm's way and back onto its feet.

WALKING IN THREES

Insects walk by moving three legs at a time—one on one side, and two on the other. This makes their bodies zigzag as they move along.

ROWING ALONG

The lesser water boatman has flattened back legs fringed with hairs. It uses these to push itself along. This species swims right side up, but some water boatmen swim upside down.

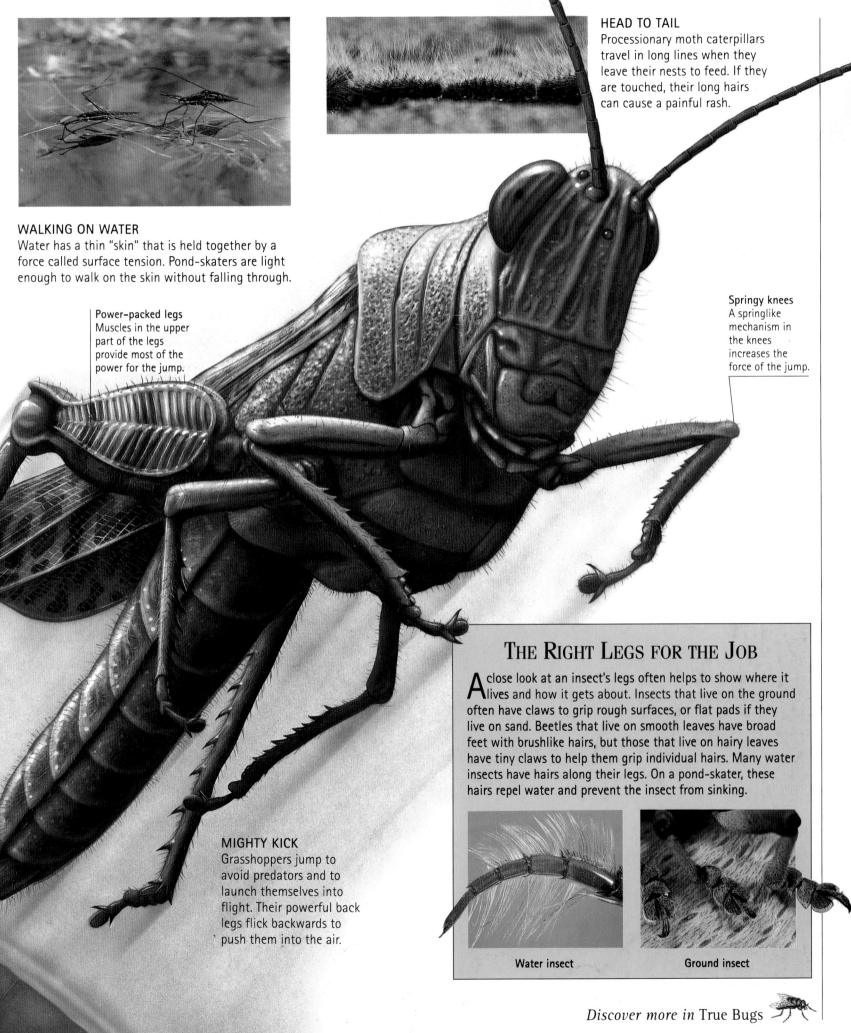

WALKING ON WATER
Water has a thin "skin" that is held together by a force called surface tension. Pond-skaters are light enough to walk on the skin without falling through.

HEAD TO TAIL
Processionary moth caterpillars travel in long lines when they leave their nests to feed. If they are touched, their long hairs can cause a painful rash.

Springy knees
A springlike mechanism in the knees increases the force of the jump.

Power-packed legs
Muscles in the upper part of the legs provide most of the power for the jump.

MIGHTY KICK
Grasshoppers jump to avoid predators and to launch themselves into flight. Their powerful back legs flick backwards to push them into the air.

THE RIGHT LEGS FOR THE JOB

A close look at an insect's legs often helps to show where it lives and how it gets about. Insects that live on the ground often have claws to grip rough surfaces, or flat pads if they live on sand. Beetles that live on smooth leaves have broad feet with brushlike hairs, but those that live on hairy leaves have tiny claws to help them grip individual hairs. Many water insects have hairs along their legs. On a pond-skater, these hairs repel water and prevent the insect from sinking.

Water insect

Ground insect

Discover more in True Bugs

Making Contact

In every insect's life, there are times when it has to make contact with other members of its species. It may need to warn of danger, to attract a mate, or to prove that it is not an enemy but a friend. Many insects communicate by sight, and they often use bright colours or patterns to identify themselves. After dark, most insects are hard to see, but fireflies are easy to spot. They make their own light, and flash coded signals to one another through the dark. For crickets, cicadas and some smaller insects, sound provides a way to contact a mate. Unlike sight, sound works during the day and night, and allows an insect to stay hidden while it broadcasts its call. Insects often use touch and taste to communicate when they meet, but they can also make contact by smell. Some of their scents waft a long way through the air, while others mark the ground to show where they have been.

LIGHTS IN THE NIGHT
Fireflies are small beetles that make contact using a pale-greenish light. The males flash as they fly overhead and the females—which are often wingless—flash back from the ground.

Male firefly

Female firefly

THE HONEYBEE DANCE

When a worker honeybee finds a good food source, it returns to the hive to pass on the news. It tells the other honeybees the distance and location of the food through a special figure-of-eight dance. If the food is far away from the hive, the honeybee does a waggle in the middle of the figure of eight (as shown below). The speed of the waggle tells the honeybees how far they must fly to find the food. The angle of the waggle shows the honeybees where the food is in relation to the sun.

Angle

Food

Waggle

Hive

SCENTED MOTH
The male tiger moth attracts females by a scent called a pheromone, which is released into the air by two glands in the abdomen. These fold away when not in use.

SOUND SIGNALS
A grasshopper calls by scraping its back legs against the hard edges of its front wings. This causes the wings to vibrate and make a sound. This process is called stridulation.

TOUCH AND TASTE
When two ants meet, they touch each other briefly with their antennae. This tells them if they are from the same nest, and passes on the taste of any food they have found.

DID YOU KNOW?
The male mole cricket attracts mates with one of the loudest calls in the insect world. The cricket makes his call by rubbing his front wings together, and his Y-shaped burrow amplifies the sound. In still air, it can be heard more than 800 m (1/2 mile) away.

DANCING LIGHTS
Each species of firefly produces a different sequence of flashes. The flashes work like messages in Morse code, and ensure that males are attracted to the right species of mate.

33

Butterflies and Moths

COLOURED SCALES
The scales on a butterfly's wings overlap like tiles on a roof. They often reflect light in a special way that produces brilliant colours.

Butterflies are the most eye-catching members of the insect world, while moths are often quite dull. Yet despite their differences in colour, these insects are closely related and have many features in common.
Butterflies and moths spend the first part of their lives as caterpillars. They change shape during a resting stage as a pupa (left), and emerge as adults with wings covered with tiny scales. Unlike caterpillars, an adult butterfly or moth eats liquid food, such as nectar or rotting fruit. It does this with a sucking tube called a proboscis, which coils up when the insect is not using it. Butterflies fly by day, but most moths fly at dusk or after dark, and spend the day hidden on leaves or trees. There are more than 150,000 species of butterfly and moth. The largest have wingspans of more than 25 cm (10 in), but the smallest, called pygmy moths, are not much bigger than a fingernail.

I SPY
Most moths use camouflage to protect them during the day. When this moth from Borneo rests on a tree, it seems to disappear.

Hercules moth caterpillar

Orchard butterfly caterpillar

SURVIVAL KIT
Caterpillars have many enemies, so they defend themselves with poisonous chemicals, irritating hairs, and inflatable "horns" that release an unpleasant smell.

Silk moth caterpillar

FLY-BY-NIGHTS

Many night-time insects are attracted to bright lights. They flutter around street lights, and often gather outside windows after dark. Scientists are not certain why light attracts insects in this way, although with moths, it may be that the light disrupts their navigation system. Moths probably fly in straight lines by using a distant light, such as the moon, like a fixed point on a compass. When a moth does this with a nearby light, the system does not work, because the position of the "fixed" point changes as soon as the moth flies past. As a result, the moth spirals around the light, and eventually flies into it.

TWIN TAILS
Swallowtails get their name from the long "tail" on each back wing. These large butterflies are fast and powerful fliers.

Malaysian lacewing butterfly

TIME OUT
Butterflies usually rest with their wings upright, although they often spread them when they bask in the sunshine. Moths usually rest with their wings held flat.

Yellow emperor moth

STRANGE BUT TRUE
Tear moths, from Southeast Asia, feed on the tears of large animals, such as cattle and buffaloes. Settling close to the eye, the moth drinks the tears through its long proboscis. Although they can be annoying, the moths do little harm.

BUTTERFLY OR MOTH?
Moths do not have a knob on the end of each antenna like most butterflies do. This elephant hawk moth has feathery antennae.

Discover more in A Complete Change

Bees, Wasps and Ants

PAINFUL JAB
This wasp can sting repeatedly, but once a honeybee stings, it dies. Because a honeybee sting has a barbed tip, some of its organs are torn out when it flies off.

Most insects live alone, coming together only to mate, but social insects have a very different way of life. They live in family groups and share the work necessary to survive. Social insects include all ants and termites, and many species of bee and wasp. These insects usually build nests in which they raise their young and store food. Some nests contain fewer than a dozen insects, but others can house more than a million. Inside each nest, one insect—the queen—normally lays eggs, and all the other insects are her offspring. Workers look after the eggs, find food and raise the young, and in ant and termite colonies, soldiers defend the nest against attack. Every year, some of the males and queens fly away and mate. After mating, the male dies and the queen starts building a new nest. She is soon surrounded by a growing family of her own.

SOLITARY BEE
Not all bees live together. Most live a solitary life, such as this digger bee, digging its way to an underground nest.

MAMMOTH LOAD
Leafcutter ants bite off pieces of plants, and carry them underground. Instead of eating these plant pieces, they eat the fungi that break the plants down.

Pollen stores

Drone
Drones are male bees that develop from unfertilised eggs. Their only job is to mate with new queens.

Empty cell

Drone cell
Drone pupae need larger cells than worker pupae.

Queen cell
Larvae selected to become queens are fed only royal jelly and are raised in special cells.

Open larva cell
This cell contains a newly hatched larva. Larvae are first fed royal jelly, and later pollen and honey.

DID YOU KNOW?

Bumblebees survive as far north as the polar tundra, where the summers are cool and short. Their large bodies are covered with a layer of insulating hairs, and they insulate their nests to keep their larvae warm.

HIVE OF ACTIVITY
Honeybees collect nectar and pollen from flowers, and take them back to their nests made of wax. The bees use the wax cells for raising young and storing pollen and honey.

SAFETY IN NUMBERS
South American army ants march across the forest floor, preying on any small animals in their path.

LIVING FOOD STORES

Honey ants live in dry places, where flowers bloom for just a few weeks each year. To survive the long dry season, they store food and water in a remarkable way. Some of the workers collect sugary nectar and feed it to workers that remain underground. The abdomens of these workers swell up like balloons as they fill with nectar. Enough is stored to provide the whole nest with food and water in times of drought, until the rains return and flowers bloom once more.

Honey stores
The nectar is capped with wax and the bees change it into honey.

Nectar stores

Worker
Workers are females that cannot breed. Royal jelly is produced from glands in their head.

Queen bee
A queen can live for five years, and lays up to 1,500 eggs each day.

Capped pupae cells
These capped yellow cells contain pupae, which will soon emerge as adult worker bees.

Flies

QUESTION OF SIZE
Male stalk-eyed flies use their strange eyestalks to measure each other's size. The largest male wins the right to mate with females.

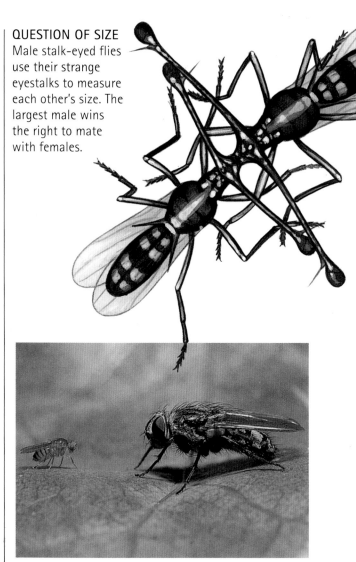

Flies are the aviation experts of the insect world. Unlike almost all other flying insects, they have only a single pair of wings, which gives them great speed and agility in the air. They also have excellent eyesight, and a pair of special stabilisers, called halteres. These keep them balanced while on the move. Altogether, there are 120,000 known species of fly. They include not only the flies that sometimes find their way indoors, but also midges and mosquitoes, brightly coloured hover flies, and many other insects that buzz noisily through the air. Although all flies eat liquid food, they do so in different ways. Some mop up fluids from flowers and fruit, or from rotting remains. Others settle on skin and use their sharp mouthparts to collect a meal of blood. Flies begin life as legless larvae, which often live inside decomposing food.

LITTLE AND LARGE
The fruit fly (left) starts life as an egg, and matures in rotting fruit. The flesh fly facing it is born live, and lives in rotting meat.

BALANCING ACT
Flies have special balancing organs called halteres, which are the modified remnants of back wings. When a crane fly lands, its halteres are easy to see.

Haltere

UPSIDE DOWN

How do houseflies land on ceilings? By using high-speed photography, scientists have learnt that they do it front-feet first. When a fly is about to land, it flies the right way up, but lifts its front legs above its body. The pads on its feet secrete an adhesive fluid, and the claws on its feet catch hold of the ceiling. The fly's body then flips upside down. Its other four legs make contact with the surface, and the fly is fastened securely. This complicated manoeuvre takes just a fraction of a second, and is much too fast for the human eye to see.

BLOOD SUCKERS
The African tsetse fly feeds on the blood of mammals, including humans. Like many blood-sucking flies, it can spread diseases as it feeds.

LAYING EGGS
Within the space of a few seconds, a female blowfly leaves a batch of eggs on some rotting remains. Her eggs will produce blind, legless larvae called maggots.

AN AERIAL COURTSHIP
Hover flies can fly forwards, backwards and sideways, and are among the few insects that are able to hover for long periods. Here, a male courts a female by hovering above her.

UP, UP AND AWAY
Like their close relatives the mosquitoes, many midges spend the first part of their life in pools and puddles. These newly emerged adult midges will soon take to the air.

STRANGE BUT TRUE
Before they mate, male dance flies present their partners with a tasty insect wrapped in silk. This gift keeps the female occupied during mating, and reduces the chance that she will attack the male. But some males cheat, and when their females unwrap the silk, they discover that there is nothing inside!

Discover more in A Closer View

True Bugs

People often use the word "bug" to mean any kind of insect, but true bugs are insects with mouthparts that pierce and suck. There are about 82,000 species of true bug, and while most live on land, some of the biggest and most ferocious live in lakes and ponds. Bugs use their piercing mouthparts to eat very different kinds of food. Some, including many water bugs, attack other animals. After stabbing them with their mouthparts, they suck out the nutritious fluids. Other bugs, including aphids, shield bugs and cicadas, live on plants and drink sugar-rich sap. Bugs hatch from eggs as nymphs, which are similar in shape to their parents. They moult up to six times before they become adults, and during this process, they often change colour. Australian harlequin bugs (above) are bright orange when adult, but orange and steely blue as nymphs.

SMELLY PREY
When threatened, stink bugs produce pungent chemicals from glands near their back legs. Many, including this specimen from Borneo, are brightly coloured to warn off birds.

WALKING ON WATER
Pond-skaters are bugs with long legs that live on the water's surface. Here, several of them are feeding on a dead insect.

SLEEP WALKERS
Bedbugs use their piercing mouthparts to feed on human blood. They are active at night, but hide away in bedding and clothes during the day. Because of modern insecticides, they are becoming less common.

SNEAK ATTACK
The back swimmer swims upside down under the water, using its long back legs as oars. It pounces on insects that fall into the water and stabs them.

PIERCING MOUTHPARTS

A bug's mouthparts are very long and form an organ called a rostrum. The rostrum contains a central tube with a sharp-tipped stylet on either side. Inside the tube are two hollow channels that carry liquids up or down. To feed, the bug pierces an animal or plant with its stylets, and then pushes the tube into the wound. It pumps saliva down one of the channels and sucks up liquid food through the other. This cicada shown above is sucking plant sap. In many bugs, the rostrum folds away against the body when not in use.

BUG FARM
When aphids feed, they produce droplets of a sugary fluid called honeydew. Ants use this as food, and in return, they protect the aphids from their enemies.

LIVING THORNS
These treehopper bugs from Florida are disguised as thorns. If predators do find them, their shape makes them hard to eat.

Discover more in Food and Feeding

41

Insect Impact

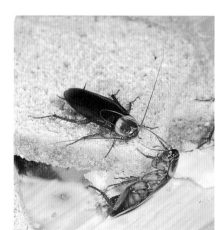

NIGHT-TIME NUISANCE
Cockroaches feed at night, and eat anything from bread to shoe polish. They are very sensitive to vibrations, and scuttle away as soon as they sense danger.

Insects can both help and harm people. Without the ceaseless work of bees and other insects, many flowers would not be pollinated, and many of the plants we grow would not produce food. Without honeybees, there would be no honey, and without predatory insects, there would be many more pests. However, many of those pests are actually insects themselves. Caterpillars, bugs and beetles attack our crops, and in some parts of the world, swarms of locusts (a single locust is shown above) sometimes descend on fields, stripping them bare in less than an hour. Weevils bore their way through stored grain, beetles and termites tunnel through wood in houses and furniture, and some insects attack farm animals. Insects also harm us more directly. Some sting, but the most dangerous by far are those that carry diseases. Houseflies and cockroaches spread germs when they walk over our food, while mosquitoes, flies and fleas can infect us with germs when they feed on our blood.

WELCOME VISITORS
Many of the fruits and vegetables we eat have to be pollinated by insects before they will start to develop. Some fruit growers keep honeybees to pollinate their plants.

POTATO MENACE
The brightly coloured Colorado beetle comes from North America. Originally, it fed on wild plants, but it now attacks potato plants in many parts of the world.

A DIET OF WOOL
The caterpillars of clothes moths often live in tiny silk bags, and feed on wool. They sometimes chew small holes in woollen clothes and blankets.

DEMOLITION SQUAD
Termites work in darkness, eating wood from the inside. The damage they cause is often hidden until the wood starts to collapse.

FATAL FLEAS
When fleas bite rats and then humans, they can pass on germs that cause the bubonic plague. In the 1300s, outbreaks of this disease killed millions of people.

THE DUNG-BEETLE STORY
Dung beetles are among our most unusual insect helpers. They dispose of animal manure (dung) by using it as food for their larvae. When early settlers imported cattle to Australia, the manure piled up, and the grass began to die. This was because Australian dung beetles were used to the droppings of native animals, but not to those of cattle. The solution to this problem was to bring in dung beetles from Africa, where wild cattle were common. Within a few years, they had cleared the manure away.

DID YOU KNOW?
The most serious disease spread by insects is malaria. It is carried by mosquitoes in their salivary glands. Since the Stone Age, malaria may have caused half of all human deaths. Today, it still kills between 2 and 4 million people every year.

MOUTHS ON THE MOVE
This swarm of hungry locusts in Africa spells disaster for farmers whose crops are in its path. Locusts normally live alone, but swarm when they are on the move.

Looking at Spiders

GIANT FANGS
These fangs stab downwards, pinning prey to the ground as the spider bites. Other spiders have fangs that come together when they bite.

With their hairy bodies and long legs, spiders provoke both fear and fascination. Like an insect, a spider has jointed legs and a hard body case, or carapace, but differs from an insect in many other ways. Spiders belong to a group of animals called arachnids, which also includes scorpions, mites and ticks. Their bodies are divided into two parts separated by a slender waist, and they have eight legs rather than six. Spiders do not have antennae or wings, but they do have many eyes, and powerful jaws that can deliver a poisonous bite. All spiders are predators. Some eat frogs, lizards and even small birds, but most feed on insects. A spider uses its poisonous fluid, or venom, to paralyse its prey, and then injects it with digestive juices to dissolve the prey's tissue. The spider can then slowly suck it up. About 35,000 species of spider have been identified. They live in many different habitats, including forests, grasslands, caves, fresh water and our homes.

WATCHING FOR PREY
Most spiders have poor eyesight and sense the movement of prey through the hairs that cover their body and legs. This jumping spider however, has unusually good vision.

Leg
Each of a spider's eight legs is attached to the cephalothorax.

HOW SPIDERS MOULT

In order to grow, spiders must periodically moult, or shed their hard outer skin. Just before it starts to moult, a spider hangs upside down and secures itself with a silk thread. Its skin splits around the sides of its cephalothorax and abdomen, and starts to fall away. Meanwhile, the spider pulls its legs out of the old skin, just like someone pulling their fingers out of a glove. When its body is free, it hangs from the thread, and expands to its new size.

Skin splits

Legs pull out

Skin dries and hardens

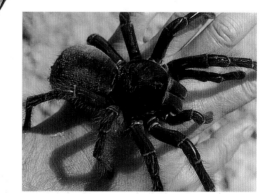

BIRD KILLER
The largest spider in the world is the bird-eating spider, or tarantula, from South America. It can be as wide as 28 cm (11 inches).

Abdomen
This relatively soft part of the body contains the spider's heart, gut, lungs and the glands that produce silk.

Cephalothorax
This consists of the head and thorax. Its upper surface is protected by a shieldlike carapace.

DID YOU KNOW?
Some spiders have such bad eyesight that they cannot find an insect that is right in front of them. But if the insect moves, the spider will immediately sense the vibrations it creates, and pounce with deadly accuracy.

Eyes
Although most spiders have eight eyes in two rows, their vision is poor.

Pedipalp
Spiders use these leglike body parts to touch and taste. During mating, males transfer sperm through the pedipalps.

Breathing pores
Spiders breathe with small lungs. Many also have air tubes, or tracheae.

Jaw
Each jaw ends in a hollow fang that releases venom. Spiders use their jaws for attack and defence, and sometimes for digging burrows.

A SPIDER'S SHAPE
Although they vary greatly in size, spiders are quite similar in shape. A spider's abdomen is usually rounded, but in a few species it is flattened with spiky edges.

Underside view of a spider

SPIDERS IN WATER
Some spiders live on top of fresh water. They hunt prey on the water surface, in water, and on land. Sometimes these spiders are eaten by fish.

Claws
Spiders use these to cling onto rough surfaces and to walk among the silk threads in their webs.

Spinnerets
Silk emerges from the small nozzles on the spinnerets.

45

Silk and Web Makers

Silk is a remarkable substance, made by all spiders and some insects. It starts out as a liquid, but can be turned into elastic strands that are sometimes stronger than steel. Spiders make different kinds of silk in special glands in their abdomens. The glands are connected to nozzles called spinnerets. As the liquid silk emerges from its spinnerets, a spider tugs it with its legs, which hardens the silk. For many spiders, the most important use of silk is in making webs. The shape of the web and the time spent building it depend on the species of spider. Once a web is complete, spiders usually lie in wait, either on the web itself or close enough to touch it with their legs. If anything makes the web vibrate, the spider instantly rushes out to investigate. If it discovers something edible, the spider often wraps up the victim with sticky threads before delivering a deadly bite.

FOOD PARCEL
This orb-web spider has caught a ladybird. To make sure victims cannot escape, they are wrapped in silk, which also prevents stinging insects from fighting back.

Hunting spider

Web-building spider

DIFFERENT FEET
Spiders that hunt their prey usually have two claws on each foot, while spiders that trap their prey in webs have three. The central claw closes to grip the web.

COMMUNAL WEBS
In warm parts of the world, some spiders cooperate to catch prey. This giant web in Papua New Guinea is several metres long. It was built by many spiders working together.

SPINNING SILK
Most spiders have three or four pairs of spinnerets. Here, several spinnerets work together as a spider builds its web.

OTHER USES OF SILK

Silk has many uses apart from making webs and wrapping up prey. Many spiderlings use silk to help them leave the nest and most spiders use it to produce a dragline, a thin silk thread that trails behind them as they move. With a dragline the spiders can lower themselves through the air, but winch themselves back up if they do not like what they find. Spiders also use silk for protecting their eggs and, as shown here, for making shelters. This jumping spider has used silk to fasten two leaves together as a temporary shelter.

PORTABLE TRAP
A net-throwing spider hangs upside down holding its web with its legs. If an insect walks beneath it, the spider stretches and lowers the web to scoop up the prey.

TAILOR-MADE TRAPS

Spiders' webs vary from extremely precise structures to untidy tangles of silk threads. Many spiders look after their webs carefully, repairing any damage promptly.

Sheet web
Sheet-web spiders spin a maze of webs to trap their prey.

Orb web
Orb weavers spin a spiral of silk that is covered with sticky droplets.

Triangle web
Triangle spiders hold their webs taut, but release them to entangle prey.

FUNNEL WEB

Funnel-web spiders build a web against rocks or plants and wait at the funnel entrance to grab insects that fall on the web.

The Hunters

Not all spiders catch their prey with webs. Many use traps of a different kind, while others set off on patrol and pounce on anything that could make a meal. Spiders that trap their prey rely on disguise for a successful ambush. Crab spiders, for example, camouflage themselves and catch insects that land within reach. Trappers also include many species that build silk tubes, or tunnels with secret doors. If an unsuspecting insect wanders nearby, a trap-door spider flings open the door and lunges at its prey. Spiders that search for food operate either by day or by night. The busiest daytime hunters are the jumping spiders. They have extra-large eyes to help them find their prey. When the sun sets, the jumping spiders hide away, and much larger and more sinister-looking spiders, such as tarantulas, begin to emerge. Instead of hunting by sight, these spiders hunt by touch.

HIDDEN HUNTERS
Camouflaged crab spiders keep quite still as they lurk among flowers with their front legs wide open. If a meal, such as a honeybee, lands within range, they strike instantly.

DEATH TRAP
This trap-door spider has opened its door wide, revealing the burrow beneath. Some trap doors are light and flimsy, but others contain earth as well as silk, and close under their own weight.

SLIPPERY CATCH
Raft spiders hunt water animals by sensing the ripples the prey creates. After stabbing a fish with its fangs, this spider hauls its catch ashore.

STRANGE BUT TRUE
At dusk, the bolas spider twirls a thread that ends in a drop of liquid silk. Male moths are attracted by a chemical in the silk, and become caught on the sticky blob. The spider then hauls in its prey.

JUMPING ON PREY
Trailing its dragline, this sequence shows a jumping spider leaping through the air. This hunter can jump four times the length of its own body.

HUNTING UNDERWATER

The water spider survives in its unusual habitat by making a silk bubble, as shown below, to store air. It sits inside the air bubble and waits for prey to come along. If a small animal comes within range, the spider dashes out, attacks, and brings the victim back into the air bubble to be eaten. Water spiders also catch animals that have fallen onto the surface of the water, as well as search out prey on the muddy bottom of a pond. They find most of their food by detecting vibrations in the water.

NIGHT STALKERS
This rearing tarantula is more than a match for a mouse. Its diet can also include frogs, lizards, small birds and even young snakes.

Discover more in Predators and Parasites

INVISIBLE SPIDER
This Australian spider rests with its body sideways across a twig. Its dappled colours and knobbly abdomen make it look just like a ridge of bark.

ANT IMPOSTER
Many animals avoid ants because they can bite and sting. However, a close look shows that this tropical "ant" has eight legs. It is a spider in disguise.

PROTECTING EGGS
This spider (in the centre) camouflages its egg sacs by disguising them as wrapped up prey. Other animals will be less interested in dead remains than in a spider's living eggs.

• SPOTLIGHT ON SPIDERS •

Spider Defence

Spiders are very effective hunters, but sometimes they can become the hunted. Their enemies are numerous, and include birds, lizards, frogs, toads, centipedes and deadly hunting wasps. These wasps paralyse spiders by stinging them, and use the still-living spider as food for their young. To outwit their enemies, spiders use a range of defences. Many are camouflaged to blend in with their backgrounds, while some imitate things that are not normally eaten. Others hide away in burrows topped with trap doors, and hold their doors firmly shut if an enemy tries to break in. If this tactic fails and the door is forced open, the owner often retreats into a hidden chamber behind a further door. It remains here until the danger has passed. Despite these defences, many spiders are killed. Their best resource in the struggle for survival, however, is that most species lay a large number of eggs, so although many die, some always manage to survive.

NASTY SHOWER
A tarantula's hairs have microscopic barbed spines that can make skin itch and burn. When threatened, a tarantula scrapes hairs off its abdomen and showers them on its enemy.

EGG FACTORY
A single garden spider can produce more than 500 eggs. Garden spiders live in the open and are easy prey, so only a few of the spiderlings survive to become adults.

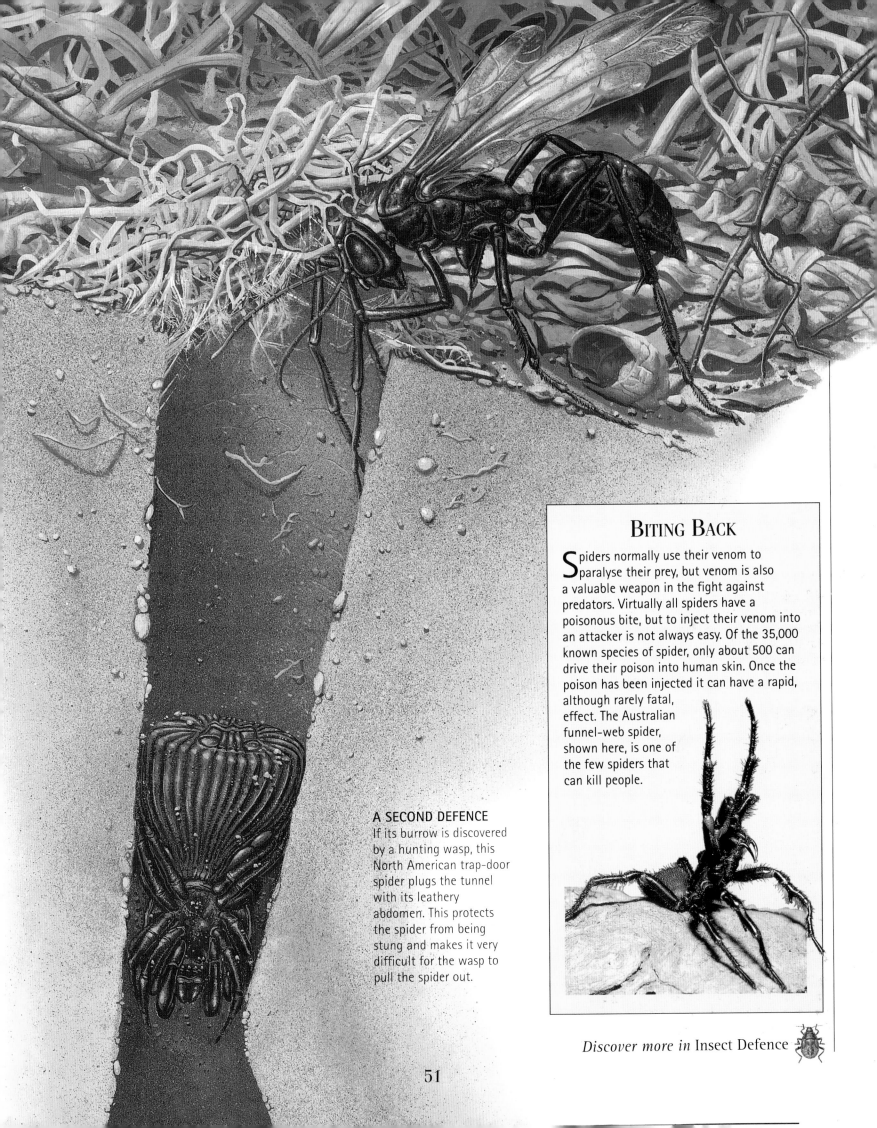

BITING BACK

Spiders normally use their venom to paralyse their prey, but venom is also a valuable weapon in the fight against predators. Virtually all spiders have a poisonous bite, but to inject their venom into an attacker is not always easy. Of the 35,000 known species of spider, only about 500 can drive their poison into human skin. Once the poison has been injected it can have a rapid, although rarely fatal, effect. The Australian funnel-web spider, shown here, is one of the few spiders that can kill people.

A SECOND DEFENCE
If its burrow is discovered by a hunting wasp, this North American trap-door spider plugs the tunnel with its leathery abdomen. This protects the spider from being stung and makes it very difficult for the wasp to pull the spider out.

Discover more in Insect Defence

New Life

Before spiders can reproduce, males and females have to come together to mate. For a male, mating can be a dangerous activity, because he needs to be cautious to avoid being attacked by the female. Once mating has taken place, the male's work is done. Maternal care varies between different species of female spider. However, they all wrap their eggs in a silk parcel called an egg sac, and either hide the sac somewhere safe, or carry it with them as they hunt. Young spiders, or spiderlings, look like miniature versions of their parents. They break out of the egg sac soon after they hatch, and at first cling either to each other, or to their mother's body. A few female spiders find food for their young, but eventually they have to catch food for themselves. From then on each spiderling is on its own.

BREAKING OUT
Most spiderlings moult for the first time while still safe inside the egg sac. After moulting, they break through the silk into the world outside.

HITCHING A RIDE
A female wolf spider's egg sac is attached to her spinnerets, and she often warms it in the sunshine (above left). When her spiderlings hatch, they climb onto the top of her abdomen.

LONG LIFE
Guarded by their mother, young tarantulas explore the outside world. Tropical tarantulas are the longest living of all spiders.

TREADING LIGHTLY

Most spiders live alone and do not like to be approached. This creates problems for male spiders, because they could be attacked when they try to court females. The males avoid this fate by using signals. In species that have good eyesight, the male waves its legs or its pedipalps in a special sequence. Web-building spiders often have poor eyesight, so the male (far left) has to use another signaling technique. This spider tugs on the female's web as it carefully makes its approach.

UNEQUAL PARTNERS
Many male spiders are much smaller than the female. Here a male spider hesitantly advances towards his gigantic, and perhaps hungry, mate.

SECURITY BLANKET
Orb-weaving spiders often cover their egg sac with a blanket of tough silk. This makes it more difficult for predators and parasites to reach the eggs.

FLYING AWAY
To leave the nest, many species of spider use threads of silk as sails to launch themselves into the wind from the tops of plants (far left). When moving around the plants, the spiderlings use draglines as shown below.

Q: How do many spiders leave the nest?

STRANGE BUT TRUE
Many female spiders die after they have laid their eggs. For some spiderlings, the mother's body is their first meal. They feed on her remains before setting off to catch food for themselves.

Orders of Insects & Spiders

Scientists arrange living things in groups to show how they are related through evolution. The largest groups are called kingdoms, and the smallest are called species. In between, there are classes, orders, suborders, families and genera. Each species consists of living things that breed together, and each one has its own two-part scientific name. So far, scientists have identified and named more than 2 million species of living things. Of these, only about 45,000 are vertebrates (animals with backbones) while more than 1 million are arthropods, which include insects and spiders. The species totals shown on these two pages are recent estimates, but it is certain that many more insects and spiders await discovery.

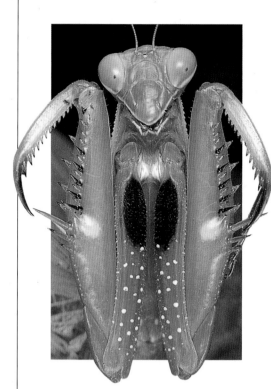

READY TO STRIKE
With its stabbing forelegs raised and ready to strike, this mantis looks like someone at prayer. It belongs to the order Mantodea.

TWO WINGS
Like all other species in the order Diptera, this greenbottle fly has just a single pair of wings. It is a fast and noisy flier.

INSECTS
Class: Insecta

Main insect orders	Meaning of order name	Estimated no. of species	Examples
Coleoptera	hard wings	400,000	beetles, cockchafers, fireflies, ladybirds, weevils
Lepidoptera	scaly wings	150,000	butterflies, moths
Hymenoptera	membrane wings	130,000	ants, bees, wasps
Diptera	two wings	120,000	true flies, hover flies, midges, mosquitoes
Hemiptera	half wings	82,000	aphids, bugs, cicadas, pond-skaters, water boatmen, back swimmers, water scorpions
Orthoptera	straight wings	20,500	crickets, grasshoppers, locusts
Trichoptera	hairy wings	10,000	caddis flies
Collembola	sticky peg	6,000	springtails
Odonata	toothed flies	5,500	damselflies, dragonflies
Neuroptera	net-veined wings	5,000	lacewings
Thysanoptera	fringed wings	5,000	thrips
Blattodea	insect avoiding light	3,700	cockroaches
Pscoptera	milled wings	3,200	booklice, woodlice
Phthiraptera	louse wings	3,000	biting and sucking lice
Phasmatodea	like a ghost	2,500	leaf insects, stick insects
Siphonaptera	tube without wings	2,400	fleas
Isoptera	equal wings	2,300	termites
Ephemeroptera	living for a day	2,100	mayflies
Plecoptera	wickerwork wings	2,000	stoneflies
Dermaptera	leathery wings	1,800	earwigs
Mantodea	like a prophet	1,800	praying mantises
Mecoptera	long wings	400	scorpion flies
Thysanura	bristle tails	370	silverfish

BITING JAWS
These formidable jaws that bite downwards belong to a mygalomorph spider, which is a member of the suborder Orthognatha.

TRUE SPIDERS
These sideways-biting jaws belong to a true spider, from the suborder Labidognatha. This large group includes the vast majority of the world's spiders.

SPIDERS
Class: Arachnida

Spider order
Araneae

Suborder	Distinctive features	No. of families	Estimated no. of species	Examples and family name
Labidognatha (true spiders)	Their jaws are attached below the head and bite from side to side.	90	32,000	jumping spiders (Salticidae) sheet-web weavers (Linyphiidae) orb weavers (Argiopidae) wolf spiders (Lycosidae) crab spiders (Thomisidae) funnel-web spiders (Agelenidae)
Orthognatha (mygalomorph spiders)	Their jaws bite forwards and down.	15	3,000	tarantulas (Theraphosidae)
Mesothelae (primitive, segmented spiders)	Their abdomens have several segments, like those of insects.	1	24	segmented spiders (Liphistiidae)

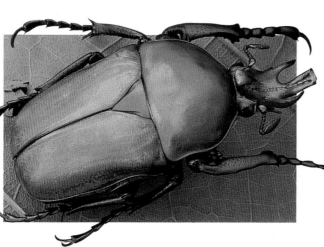

HARD WINGS
This scarab beetle belongs to the biggest order, Coleoptera. Its back wings are protected by hard front wings when it clambers across the ground.

SCALY WINGS
This birdwing butterfly belongs to the order Lepidoptera. Its wings and body are covered with a huge number of tiny, but brightly coloured scales.

STRAIGHT WINGS
Bush crickets belong to the order Orthoptera. Like grasshoppers, they have straight wings, and the front pair is often hard and leathery.

Index

Picture Credits

(t=top, b=bottom, l=left, r=right, c=centre, F=front, C=cover, B=back, Bg=background)
Ardea, 42c (I.R. Beames), 30bl (J. Daniels), 34br (A. Warren). **Kathie Atkinson**, 26bl, 45bl, 50tl. **Auscape**, 9tl (K. Atkinson), 36c, (J. Cancalosi), 40tl, 46cr, 55bc (J.P. Ferrero), 14tl, 31br, 52cr, 55cl, 55tl (P. Goetgheluck P.H.O.N.E.), 42/43c (Helio/Van Ingen), 23tcr, (C.A. Henley), 23bcr, 28bl (R. Morrison), 27bl (A. & J. Six), 54bl (J. Six), 55cr (G. Threlfo). **Austral International**, 36tl (R. Amann/Sygma), 44br (D. Heuclin/SIPA Press), 16bc, 31bl (H. Pfletschinger/Camera Press). **Australian Picture Library**, 46br (M. Moffett/Minden Pictures). **Dr Hans Bänziger**, 35br. **Bruce Coleman Limited**, 29tr (J. Brackenbury), 16tl, 18bl, 47br, 52bl (J. Burton), 41bl (J. Cancalosi), 50br (R.P. Carr), 25tl (G. Dore), 44cl (F. Labhardt), 28br (Dr E. Pott), 51br (F. Prenzel), 27c (Dr S. Prato), 32c, 46bl, 54tl (Dr F. Sauer), 44tr, 52tr (A. Stillwell), 19bl, 20cl, 23tr, 23br, 41br, 48bc (K. Taylor). **CSIRO Division of Entomology**, 42r (J. Green), 13b (Melbourne University Press). **Ellis Nature Photography**, 40cl. **Pavel German**, 50tc. **Mantis Wildlife**, 11cr, 24l, 26cl, 37tr, 41tr (D. Clyne), 52br (J. Frazier). **Mary Evans Picture Library**, 43tc. **NHM Picture Library**, 6tr, 6bl, 11tc

(The Natural History Museum, London). **NHPA**, 14c, 22tl (A. Bannister), 38cl, 50bl (G.I. Bernard), 32br (S. Dalton). **Oxford Scientific Films**, 9br, 22tcl, 49r (G.I. Bernard), 17tl (S. Camazine), 37tl, 43tl, 50bc, 53tl (J.A.L. Cooke), 21cr, 48cl (D. Fox). 15tr, 31tl (London Scientific Films), 48bl (A. Ramage), 6br (D. Shale). **Nature Focus**, 10br, 11tr (Australian Museum). **Charles Palek**, 6tl. **The Photo Library, Sydney**, 14bcr, 30tr, 39tr (Dr J. Burgess/SPL), 24tr (C. Cooper), 38bc (M. Dohrm/SPL),10bl, 14br, 14bl, 20tl (Nuridsany & Perennou/SPL), 34tr, (A. Pasieka/SPL), 21tl (J.H. Robinson), 8br, 13tr, 14bcl, 40bl D. Scharf/SPL), 18c (SPL), 11tl (A. Syred/SPL). **Planet Earth Pictures**, 42bc (J. Downer), 35bl, 40c (G. du Feu), 11bl, 36bl, 46tr, (S. Hopkin), 16br, 21tr (B. Kenney), 23tl (K. Lucas), 12bc, 12br (J. Lythgoe), 42tr (J. & G. Lythgoe), 18cl (D. Maitland). **Premaphotos Wildlife**, 17tr, 20bl, 22bl, 34c, 38c, 50cl (K.G. Preston-Mafham). **Terra Australis Photo Agency**, 31tr, 39br (E. Beaton).

Illustration Credits

Susanna Addario, 3, 30tl, 30cr, 30br, 36/37b, 36tr. **Martin Camm**, 18tl, 18br, 19t. **Simone End**, 1, 7br, 7bc, 29br, 29bc, 29bl, icons. **Christer**

Eriksson, 5br, 6/7c, 15br, 16bl, 28/29c, 30/31c, 48/49c, 55tr. **Giuliano Fornari**, 46cl, 47c, 47cr, 47tr, 47tcr. **Jon Gittoes**, 40/41c. **Ray Grinaway**, 4tl, 5tl, 5cr, 7c, 14tc, 14cl, 15tl, 28/29t, 28cl, 28c (J. Brackenbury/Cassell), 34bl, 34tcl, 34bcl, 34tl, 38bl, 48tl, 48c. **Tim Hayward/Bernard Thornton Artists, UK**, 22/23c, 22c, 52/53c, 52cl. **Robert Hynes**, 20/21c, 21br. **David Kirshner**, 8/9c, 8bl, 9tr, 10/11c. **Frank Knight**, 26/27t, 27br. **James McKinnon**, 50/51c. **John Richards**, 32/33c, 32bc, 32bcl, 32cl, 32tl, 33b. **Trevor Ruth**, 2, 34/35c, 35tr, 35cr, 38tl, 38/39c. **Claudia Saraceni**, 4/5bc, 16/17c, 17r, 42tl, 42bl, 43bl. **Kevin Stead**, 4bl, 5tr, 12/13c, 12l, 13r, 19br, 24/25c, 24b, 25tc, 25tcl, 25tr, 32bl. **Thomas Trojer**, 44/45c, 44bl, 45br. **Rod Westblade**, endpapers.

Cover Credits

Susanna Addario, BCbr. **Martin Camm**, FCtl. **Richard Davies**, Bg. **Christer Eriksson**, FCtr, FCbc. **David Kirshner**, BCtl.